THE TRUTH ABOUT CARBON MONOXIDE POISONING

BY MATTHEW E. MAZUR, JR. ESQ.

Copyrighted Material

Copyright 2019

Matthew Mazur, P.A. – All Rights Reserved.

All rights Reserved. No part of this publication or the information in it may be quoted from or reproduced in any form by means such as printing, scanning, photocopying or otherwise without prior written permission of the copyright holder. All images are licensed acquired or original images and remain with their respective owners. Front Cover Illustration 142307247 © Lkeskinen0 - Dreamstime.com

Have a question or concern? Contact info@mazur-law.com.

Copyrighted Material

THIS BOOK IS FOR EDUCATIONAL PURPOSES ONLY. THIS BOOK IS NOT LEGAL ADVICE!!!

The Florida bar requires that I inform you what is in this book is **<u>not legal advice</u>**. I am not your attorney until you and I enter into a written agreement for me to be your attorney. This book should not be taken in any way, shape or form to be advice about your specific case, as each case is different, and an attorney can only give you quality legal advice when he or she understands the specific facts involved in your case. Matthew Mazur, P.A. specifically disclaim any liability incurred by the direct use or indirect use of the contents of this book. This book was written to provide you with educational information only.

CONTENTS

Forward

Chapter I - What Is Carbon Monoxide & Carbon Monoxide Poisoning? 1

CHAPTER II - How Does Carbon Monoxide Poisoning Happen? 2

CHAPTER III - What Are The Symptoms Of Carbon Monoxide Poisoning? 5

CHAPTER IV - Are There Medical Treatments For Carbon Monoxide Poisoning? 11

CHAPTER V - What Can Be Done To Prevent Carbon Monoxide Poisoning? 13

CHAPTER VI - What To Do If You Suspect You Have Been Poisoned By Carbon Monoxide? 16

CHAPTER VII - How Do You Know If You Have A Carbon Monoxide Poisoning lawsuit? 19

CHAPTER VIII - What Is The Legal Process Like For A Carbon Monoxide Poisoning Lawsuit? 22

CHAPTER IX - Before You Make An Appointment For That "Free Consultation" 24

CHAPTER X - What Cases Do You Not Accept? 26

CHAPTER XI - The Eight Biggest Mistakes You Can Make That Will Poison Your Case 29

CHAPTER XII - Internet Resources On Carbon Monoxide 35

Poisoning
About Our Firm

FOREWARD

Why This Book?

I wrote this book because, if you are like most people dealing with Carbon Monoxide Poisoning of yourself or a loved one, you have a lot of questions and not many answers. For many of you this may be the first time in your life that you have had to deal with a catastrophic medical condition. It is a scary time, one in which you feel like you are alone. This book will hopefully provide you with information to make informed decisions and take control of your situation.

It is likely that you have started your search for an attorney if you believe the circumstances of your Carbon Monoxide Poisoning was the result of someone else's negligence. You most likely have found that the majority of attorney advertising you have run into does not give you any useful information about your situation. It typically is all about the attorney and why you should hire them, not about you, your situation, and what you want to know before you hire any attorney. A lot of ads will say "Hire Me, we don't charge a fee unless we get you money," but then you realize that ALL personal injury attorneys say that. You also begin to realize that most attorneys advertise that they "care for you" or "are aggressive," which is 100% meaningless. Don't you expect that the attorney that you eventually hire will care about you and your family? That they will be aggressive. A lot of what you will see is hype and will not help you make an informed decision about who you should hire to represent you or a loved one that has been poisoned by Carbon Monoxide.

I wrote this book for YOU. So that you could have good information on Carbon Monoxide Poisoning that could be reviewed in the privacy of your own home without any pressure to hire an attorney. The last thing that you need at this time is some attorney pressuring you to retain them. You need time to understand your situation and make informed decisions. This book is the first step for you to take to gain control of your situation and make informed decisions that will best impact your future. Regardless of whether or not you retain my law firm or another law firm, it is our sincerest hope that this book helped you make the best decision for you and your loved ones.

CHAPTER I

What Is Carbon Monoxide & Carbon Monoxide Poisoning?

Carbon Monoxide is an odorless, colorless, tasteless gas that is produced by the incomplete combustion of fossil fuels. Carbon monoxide was first described in a scientific context by Arnaldus de Villa Nova, a Spanish doctor in the 11th Century. Carbon monoxide forms in preference to the more usual carbon dioxide when there is a reduced availability of oxygen present during the combustion process. In 1776, the French Chemist de Lassone created Carbon Monoxide by heating zinc oxide with coke. It has the molecular formula of CO. A Carbon Monoxide molecule consists of a carbon atom bonded to an oxygen atom. Carbon Monoxide was first identified as a compound containing carbon and oxygen by William Cumberland Cruikshank, an English chemist in 1800. Carbon Monoxide is toxic. The toxic aspects of Carbon Monoxide gas was first investigated by the French physiologist Claude Bernard around 1846. Carbon Monoxide at high levels can kill a person in minutes

The Centers for Disease Control estimates that carbon monoxide poisoning claims nearly 500 lives, and causes more than 15,000 visits to hospital emergency departments annually. Carbon Monoxide Poisoning is the most common type of fatal poisoning in the United States. Exposure to Carbon Monoxide can cause damage to the central nervous system and the heart. Following a significant exposure to Carbon Monoxide an individual can suffer long-term effects that last a life time. Carbon Monoxide can also have severe effects on the fetus of a pregnant woman. Despite its serious toxic nature, Carbon Monoxide plays a highly useful role in modern technology, being a precursor for a whole host of products.

CHAPTER II

How Does Carbon Monoxide Poisoning Happen?

Carbon Monoxide Poisoning can happen as a result of many different activities. The most common sources of Carbon Monoxide Poisoning today are motor vehicle exhaust, smoke from fires, engine fumes, and nonelectric heaters. Carbon monoxide poisoning typically occurs as a result of malfunctioning or obstructed exhaust systems.

Potential Sources of Carbon Monoxide:

• Gas water heaters	• Propane-fueled forklifts
• Kerosene space heaters	• Gasoline powered tools
• Charcoal grills	• Indoor tractor pulls
• Propane heaters and stoves	• Boat engines
• Gasoline, Propane, and diesel powered generators	• Spray paint, solvents, degreasers, and paint removers

Risks for Carbon Monoxide Poisoning include:

- Riding in the back of enclosed pickup trucks
- Working at pulp mills and steel foundries
- Being involved in Fire Rescue Activities
- Using heating sources or electric generators during power outages
- Working indoors with combustion engines or combustible gases
- Swimming near or under the stern or swim-step of a boat with the boat engine running
- Back drafting when a boat is operated at a high bow

- angle
- Mooring next to a boat that is running a generator or engine
- Improper boat ventilation

It can happen in the home, when a gas stove, boiler, water heater or other appliance is not properly installed or maintained. If it is not vented properly, exhaust containing carbon monoxide can be released into the home and cause Carbon Monoxide Poisoning. It is important that you have regular maintenance and inspection of gas stove, boilers, water heaters, and other appliances that could be sources for carbon monoxide in your home. It is vitally as important that you install Carbon Monoxide Detectors in your home. An ounce of prevention can save you and your family from death or a life of constant pain resulting from Carbon Monoxide Poisoning.

Carbon Monoxide Poisoning can happen at work, when combustion powered vehicles or generators are used in poorly ventilated areas. If the Carbon Monoxide is allowed to build up over time anyone within those areas is at risk of Carbon Monoxide Poisoning. It is important that you are aware of your surroundings and what machines and devices are operating around you. A common cause of Carbon Monoxide Poisoning is the use of gas or propane powered forklifts in warehouses. If such vehicles are going to be used within an enclosed space, there needs to be enough ventilation to prevent the build of Carbon Monoxide. It is very important that your employer ensures your safety by making sure there is adequate ventilation and carbon monoxide monitoring in place.

Carbon Monoxide Poisoning can happen in a vehicle or boat when the exhaust system has a leak in it and the exhaust enters the passenger compartment. The maintenance of your car or boat is very important in preventing Carbon Monoxide Poisoning. The amount of Carbon Monoxide in the passenger compartment of a car or boat can build up quickly and without you realizing you are being poisoned. The results can be deadly. Make sure that your exhaust system is maintained properly and that it is checked on a regular basis.

It only takes one significant exposure to Carbon Monoxide to change your life and the life of your family forever.

CHAPTER III

What Are The Symptoms Of Carbon Monoxide Poisoning?

The symptoms of Carbon Monoxide Poisoning are very ordinary. They can be easily confused for other medical conditions and missed by healthcare providers who are not alerted to the possibility that Carbon Monoxide Poisoning may have occurred. That is why it is important to know what is going on around your home, at work and in your vehicle or boat. If you get sick and go to the hospital make sure you raise the possibility of Carbon Monoxide Poisoning so that it is not missed by your healthcare provider.

In the winter, Carbon Monoxide Poisoning is on the minds of healthcare providers because of the use of fireplaces, heaters, and generators. However, it quickly fades from their minds once the winter season is over. Along the Gulf Coast and Atlantic Coast of the United State Carbon Monoxide Poisoning is on the minds of healthcare providers during hurricane season, again because of the use of generators after storms.

It is very important to remember that Carbon Monoxide Poisoning is not a seasonal or weather related condition, but is one that can occur at anytime and anywhere. When in doubt raise the issue with your healthcare provider so that they can run the necessary **tests to ensure that you have not been poisoned by Carbon Monoxide and they can** get you the appropriate treatment as soon as possible. There is a limited window of time within which Carbon Monoxide Poisoning can be treated. If that window is missed there is a strong likelihood that you may have long lasting effects for the rest of your life.

The symptoms of Carbon Monoxide Poison are very similar to that of the flu. Initially you may develop a slight headache, fatigue (feel tired), shortness of breath. You may even feel some nausea (like you want to throw up). You also may feel dizzy and confused. Depending upon your time of exposure these symptoms may get worse or they might go away all together after you leave the area of exposure.

If, for example, the area of exposure is in your home you may actually feel better when you get to work. The reason for this is that you are no longer being exposed to the Carbon Monoxide. You are breathing in uncontaminated air and your body is expelling the Carbon Monoxide from your system. Your organs and tissue are getting more oxygen. However, as soon as you return home, depending upon the concentration of Carbon Monoxide you will begin to develop your symptoms all over again and they may even get worse.

The following chart will give you a general idea of the symptoms you may feel at certain levels of exposure. This chart is not definitive, as each person does react differently to Carbon Monoxide at lower levels. At higher levels of exposure there is not much difference in how a person will react to being exposed to Carbon Monoxide (CO).

PPM CO in air	Percent CO in air	Symptoms experienced by healthy adults
Less than 35 ppm	0.0035%	No effect in healthy adults
100 ppm	0.01%	Slight headache, fatigue, shortness of breath, errors in judgment
200 ppm	0.02%	Headache, fatigue, nausea, dizziness
400 ppm	0.04%	Severe headache, fatigue, nausea, dizziness, confusion, can be life-threatening after 3 hours of exposure
800 ppm	0.08%	Headache, confusion, collapse, death if exposure is prolonged
1500 ppm	0.15%	Headache, dizziness, nausea,

		convulsions, collapse, death within 1 hour
3000 ppm	0.3%	Death within 30 minutes
6000 ppm	0.6%	Death within 10-15 minutes
12,000 ppm	1.2%	Nearly instant death

ppm = parts per million

How Carbon Monoxide effects an individual depends heavily on the concentration of Carbon Monoxide that individual was exposed to and the length of time of the exposure. There are two types of Carbon Monoxide Poisoning Exposures, Acute (Short Term) and Chronic (Long Term). An Acute Carbon Monoxide Poisoning is one that lasts less than 24 hours and a Chronic Carbon Monoxide Poisoning is typically viewed as being multiple exposures lasting 24 hours or more.

In an Acute Carbon Monoxide Poisoning situation, typically a person is exposed to high levels of Carbon Monoxide over a period of time (less than 24 hours) that results in significant carboxyhemoglobin concentrations in their blood. An example of an acute exposure would be when a person is driving their car and there is a leak in their exhaust system that allows high levels of carbon monoxide to build up rapidly in the passenger compartment of their car. They will develop symptoms quickly and if not removed from that environment and treated can pass out or even die.

In a Chronic Carbon Monoxide Poisoning situation (typically multiple exposures lasting 24 hours or less) a person is exposed to lower levels of the Carbon Monoxide in the air and have lower carboxyhemoglobin concentrations in their blood. An example of a Chronic Exposure would be a leaky boiler in your home. Over time the concentration levels of Carbon Monoxide would build up in your home and you would develop symptoms. The symptoms might be as benign as a mild headache and eventually build up to nausea, confusion and collapse.

Matthew E Mazur Jr.

A person suffering from Chronic Carbon Monoxide poisoning may not have the typical symptoms of an Acute Carbon Monoxide Poisoning victim, such as headache, nausea, weakness, dizziness, etc. the person suffering from Chronic Carbon Monoxide Poisoning will often be misdiagnosed as having chronic fatigue syndrome, a viral or bacterial pulmonary or gastrointestinal infection, a "run-down" condition, or immune deficiency. The problem is that lower level Carbon Monoxide Poisoning mimics the flu. Many people suffering Chronic Carbon Monoxide Exposure do not even know it is occurring and as such they do not associate their severe headache and nausea a carbon monoxide exposure. At moderate concentrations, a Carbon Monoxide Exposure can result in angina, impaired vision, and reduced brain function. At higher concentrations, carbon monoxide exposure can be fatal.

The main reason carbon monoxide is such a poisonous substance is the strength in bonding a Carbon Monoxide molecule has over Oxygen. A Carbon Monoxide molecule has at least three times the bonding ability than an oxygen molecule. What that means is that when you inhale Carbon Monoxide along with Oxygen, the Carbon Monoxide will bond to the hemoglobin in your blood three times more than the Oxygen. That will result in your body getting less oxygen than it needs. Over time this lack of oxygen will cause the cells within your body to begin to shut down and result in the symptoms discussed above.

If you suspect that you have been exposed to Carbon Monoxide and may be suffering the effects of Carbon Monoxide Poisoning it is important that your healthcare providers get you a blood test that evaluates the level of Carbon Monoxide in your blood. This blood test looks at the **CARBOXYHEMOGLOBIN** levels in your blood to determine the extent of your exposure. As discussed above carboxyhemoglobin is the result of the stronger bonding ability of Carbon Monoxide over Oxygen. The higher the concentration of your exposure the more carboxyhemoglobin there will be in your blood. The percentage of carboxyhemoglobin in your blood will provide your healthcare providers necessary information to properly treating your condition.

If you do not ask your healthcare provider to test for carboxyhemoglobin typically, they will not do so on their own. It should be done as soon as possible from the time of suspected exposure, as the signs of carbon monoxide usually leave the blood stream within hours. If you have been given oxygen by healthcare providers before the blood test is performed, the results of the test will not be accurate. This is because carboxyhemoglobin leaves the body faster when an individual is on oxygen. You should be aware of this, as even though the carboxyhemoglobin may leave your body in several hours, the damage that it causes to the brain, heart and nervous system won't.

Typically Carboxyhemoglobin has a half-life of four (4) to five (5) hours, which means that the longer after a suspected exposure you wait to get tested the less accurate the carboxyhemoglobin levels will be. The closer in time that a blood test can be run, the more accurate the test will be in determining the level of your exposure. In most cases the carboxyhemoglobin levels will drop back down to background levels (meaning normal levels not indicating an exposure) in twenty-four (24) hours.

There is some scientific research that currently suggests that a "soaking" phenomenon occurs in chronic exposures to Carbon Monoxide. Basically, what happens is that over the time of the chronic exposure, the level of carbon monoxide in a person's system increases because their body cannot remove all of the Carbon Monoxide it has ingested before being exposed to more Carbon Monoxide.

For example, if a person is working in a warehouse that is enclosed and is utilizing propane powered forklifts to move items around the warehouse, there is a strong possibility that exhaust could build up inside. If the warehouse is poorly ventilated, overtime the exhaust (including Carbon Monoxide) builds up to a point where it will start to physically impact this person. This individual while inside the warehouse will build up a certain level of Carbon Monoxide in their blood and have physical symptoms as a result of this build up. Once they leave the warehouse the concentration of carbon monoxide in their blood will start to go down and given sufficient time it will be back down to normal levels.

However, if the time away from the warehouse is not long enough, the carbon monoxide levels in the body will not go back to normal, but will remain somewhat elevated. So when they go back to work the next day, they will be starting off with elevated levels of carbon monoxide in their body and will build back up the concentration of Carbon Monoxide in their blood more rapidly once they start working in the warehouse again. As such, there will be a cumulative effect over time on the level of their carbon monoxide in their body and the damage it is causing.

Remember this is a very simplistic explanation of Carbon Monoxide Poisoning and does not provide all of the detailed information you will get from your medical providers. The purpose of the explanations in this book are to give you a basic idea of how Carbon Monoxide Poisoning occurs and what you need to watch out for to protect yourself if you find yourself being exposed to Carbon Monoxide.

It cannot be stressed enough, if you suspect that you are being exposed to Carbon Monoxide medical attention immediately! If you are noticing symptoms such as short-term memory loss, loss of balance, severe headaches, or other unusual symptoms you may have been exposed to carbon monoxide. If you believe that you have been exposed to carbon monoxide, get medical attention as soon as possible to prevent or reduce permanent damage.

CHAPTER IV

Are There Medical Treatments For Carbon Monoxide Poisoning?

There are medical treatments for Carbon Monoxide Poisoning, however there is a limited window of opportunity for this treatment. The first part of any treatment is to away from the Carbon Monoxide source. This may be your home, a vehicle or boat or where you work. By removing yourself from the Carbon Monoxide you are helping your body to recover from its effects. Depending upon your location and the knowledge of your healthcare providers there are advanced treatments available to you.

If your healthcare providers get to you within four (4) to six (6) hours of your exposure and your exposure was significant, there is a strong likelihood that they will send you for hypobaric oxygen treatment. There is scientific research that suggests that prompt treatment with hypobaric oxygen after exposure to carbon monoxide reduces the long-term impact of that exposure. Unfortunately, if you are outside of this window, it is unlikely that the hypobaric oxygen treatment will make a significant impact on your long-term prognosis.

If you have been exposed to Carbon Monoxide and are still feeling the effects, chronic headaches, fatigue, memory loss, anger issues, apathy, there are medical treatments available to help you cope with these conditions. Unfortunately, many of these conditions may be permanent if you are still suffering from them two years after your exposure. There is some medical research which indicates that Carbon Monoxide Poisoning Victims can have spontaneous recovery from some if not all of their symptoms within two years of their exposure. Unfortunately, in the cases we have seen this has not been the case.

It is very important that if you have been poisoned by Carbon Monoxide that you seek medical treatment immediately. If you are suffering lingering effects from your exposure to Carbon Monoxide you need to seek medical treatment on an ongoing basis to monitor and control your symptoms. Follow up with a doctor often following a Carbon Monoxide exposure so that you keep on top of your symptoms if they persist and get the necessary medical treatment to help you deal with those symptoms, so that you may lead as near a normal life as possible.

Unfortunately, if you have had a significant Carbon Monoxide Poisoning your life will never be the same. You will be dealing with the effects of Carbon Monoxide Poisoning for the rest of your life. The effects are also emotionally devastating to you and your family. It is important that you and your family seek counseling if the effects of your Carbon Monoxide Exposure start to impact your relationship with your spouse or children. Proper medical and psychological care over the long term is essential to maintaining a good quality of life following Carbon Monoxide Poisoning.

Do not become a victim of Carbon Monoxide twice; get the medical treatment and psychological treatment you need.

CHAPTER V

What Can Be Done To Prevent Carbon Monoxide Poisoning?

There are a few basic things that can be done to prevent Carbon Monoxide Poisoning. First and foremost, keep your boiler, water heater, stove and other appliances in good working order. Make sure that they are installed properly and are well ventilated.

If you are on the Gulf Coast or Atlantic Coast or anywhere that hurricanes are an issue, do not operate your generators inside your home or inside your garage with the garage door open. There is not enough ventilation and you are at an increased risk of Carbon Monoxide Poisoning. The same holds true for other parts of the country that deal with snow and ice storms that knock out the power. Keep the generator away from the house and out of the garage.

Planning ahead can go a long way to protect you and your family from carbon monoxide poisoning. Have a concrete slab poured with anchor points to secure your generator. Have it placed at least 10 to 20 feet away from your home, preferably in your back yard where it is more secure. Also be mindful of the placement of your generator as it relates to your neighbors, as the last thing you would want to do is cause them to suffer Carbon Monoxide Poisoning. This will give you peace of mind about the security of your generator and peace of mind as to the safety of your family and neighbors from an inadvertent exposure to Carbon Monoxide.

Install Carbon Monoxide Alarms throughout your home. Make sure that you check them regularly to ensure they are working properly and replace them as often as the manufacturer suggests. According to the National Fire Protection Association some 93% of homes have smoke alarms, yet the Consumer Product Safety Commission estimates that only 15% have carbon monoxide alarms.

A carbon monoxide monitor with an audible alarm works much like a home smoke alarm and beeps loudly when the sensors detect carbon monoxide. If the alarm sounds, evacuate the building. People who have symptoms of carbon monoxide poisoning should seek emergency medical care. Call the fire department to investigate.

You should also inspect your home for potential Carbon Monoxide hazards. Your home heating system, chimney, and flue must be inspected and cleaned by a qualified technician every year. Keep chimneys clear of bird and squirrel nests, leaves, and residue to ensure proper ventilation. Be sure your furnace and other appliances, such as gas ovens, ranges, and cook tops, are inspected for adequate ventilation. Do not burn charcoal inside your house, even inside of your fireplace. Have your gas fireplace inspected each fall to ensure the pilot light burns safely.

Do not operate gasoline-powered engines in confined areas such as garages or basements. Do not leave your car, mower, or other vehicle running in an attached garage, even with if you have the garage door open. If the wind is blowing the wrong way, it could allow the Carbon Monoxide to build up in your garage and create a potential danger to you and your family.

Make sure that the exhaust flues or ducts for appliances such as water heaters, ranges, and clothes dryers are not blocked or sealed shut, as this can create an environment for Carbon Monoxide to accumulate and become dangerous to you and your family. The cost in time and money for properly maintaining your appliances, fireplace, chimneys and Carbon Monoxide Alarms in your home is far outweighed by the devastating and long term effects Carbon Monoxide Poisoning can have on you and your family.

At work, observe your surroundings. If gas, propane or other combustion engines are going to be used make sure there is sufficient ventilation. Also make sure that there is some monitoring going on for Carbon Monoxide Levels. Just because a warehouse is big, does not mean it is ventilated enough to run gas, propane or other combustion engines inside of it. If generators are being used where you work make sure that someone has checked on the ventilation situation. You would not believe how many people will use a small generator inside to work and not even think about the exhaust. By observing your surroundings at work and making sure that your employer has thought ahead you will be protecting yourself, your fellow employees and your employer from a Carbon Monoxide tragedy.

Lastly, if you are working on your boat or car, make sure you have enough ventilation in the area you are working in. There are many tragic stories of people who have been killed working in their garages or in the engine compartment of their boat because there was not enough ventilation available. Remember concentrations of Carbon Monoxide can increase rapidly and before you know it be at such significant levels to render you incapable of recognizing or reacting to the danger posed. Be smart think before you work on your car or boat. Don't work by yourself; let someone know what you are doing. If possible have carbon monoxide monitoring to protect you from the risk of carbon Monoxide Poisoning.

Additionally, have your exhaust system checked regularly on your boat and car. The last thing you want is to have a exhaust leak expose you and your family to Carbon Monoxide when you are driving or out having fun on the lake or ocean in your boat. Prevention is the key when it comes to Carbon Monoxide Poisoning. If you take a common sense approach to your activities and what is going on around you, you will have a better chance to avoid inadvertent Carbon Monoxide Exposure and Poisoning.

Matthew E Mazur Jr.

CHAPTER VI

What To Do If You Suspect You Have Been Poisoned By Carbon Monoxide?

If you suspect that you have been exposed to Carbon Monoxide or Poisoned by Carbon Monoxide:

SEEK MEDICAL ATTENTION IMMEDIATELY!

Do not waste any time getting yourself or your family to the hospital. If you believe that the area you currently are in is the source of the exposure, get out of there immediately. If you are feeling dazed or confused call 911 and get out of the home.

Fire Departments typically have monitoring equipment that they can use to determine if a location has elevated levels of Carbon Monoxide. They will typically take such readings when there is a suspicion that Carbon Monoxide Poisoning is possible. Do not go back in and take any readings yourself.

The most important thing you can do once you believe that you have been poisoned by Carbon Monoxide is to get medical help! Go to the emergency room. Make sure that you let them know that you think you may have been exposed to Carbon Monoxide. Make sure that they do a CARBOXYHEMOGLOBIN test of you blood. This is the most definitive way to know whether or not you have been exposed to Carbon Monoxide. Remember though, that if you have been given oxygen treatment or have been outside of the area where you are being exposed to Carbon Monoxide for twenty-four (24) hours or more this test will not accurately reflect the exposure you may have received.

Once you have received medical treatment, you should make

sure that the source of your exposure has been identified so that you do end up exposing yourself again. If the Fire Department was called, chances are they already determined the source. If not, you should have the appliances in your home that may be sources of Carbon Monoxide inspected. You should immediately install Carbon Monoxide Monitors in your home to ensure that you safe there. You should have the exhaust system of your car or boat checked out to ensure that there are no leaks that may have caused your exposure. If you suspect that your exposure was at work, you need to contact your employer and let them know what happened to you. The bottom line is that it is very important that you determine the source of your Carbon Monoxide Poisoning to protect you, your family, your coworkers and friends.

Additionally, you will probably want to start keeping a journal of how you are feeling after your exposure. You need to be detailed and specific. If you are feeling tired, having headaches, feeling angry, feeling depressed etc. you need to write it down. In situations where the exposure was minor the symptoms should go away in a few days to weeks. In situations where the exposure was either significant or chronic there is a possibility that your symptoms may not go away. In those situations it will be vitally important that you know what is going on in your life so that your healthcare providers can help you deal with any long term symptoms such as headaches, depression, fatigue, etc. It will most likely be necessary to have your spouse keep a journal as well, as it is likely that they will observe changes in you that you are not aware of. In many Carbon Monoxide Poisoning cases, it is the spouse that sees the changes before the victim.

As with any medical condition the more you know about it and how it is affecting you the better you will be able to handle it. You will also be in a better position to provide your medical providers with information that will help them better treat your condition. Does not become a victim of Carbon Monoxide a second time; take control of your situation by knowing how you are being impacted on a daily basis. The time you take to track what is going on in your life following a Carbon Monoxide Poisoning event, will benefit you in better treatment by your medical care providers and a better understanding by you and your loved ones of what has happened to you. The more you know and are aware of the better you will be able to handle your situation.

CHAPTER VII

How Do You Know If You Have A Carbon Monoxide Poisoning lawsuit?

Whether or not you have a Carbon Monoxide Poisoning Lawsuit should not be your first concern. Focus first on getting the necessary medical treatment you need. Once you have gotten medical treatment, if you believe someone is responsible for your Carbon Monoxide Poisoning then take the time to look for an attorney to represent you.

If you suffered Carbon Monoxide Poisoning as a result of a boiler, stove, water heater or other appliance in your home, the first question that you should ask yourself is was this appliance maintained? Who was responsible for maintaining this appliance? Many times the person responsible for maintaining the appliance is the person who suffered Carbon Monoxide Poisoning. In those cases the responsible party is the one you see in the mirror. However, if you had a contract with a service company to maintain that appliance or boiler they may be responsible for the Carbon Monoxide Poisoning event.

Additionally, if you are a renter and the landlord is responsible for maintaining the appliances, boiler or water heater they may be responsible for the Carbon Monoxide Poisoning event. In both of these cases whether or not someone else was legally responsible for you being poisoned by Carbon Monoxide will come down to whether or not they owed you a legal duty. In the case of your landlord, were they legally responsible to maintain the boiler or water heater? In the case of the service company you hired to maintain your water heater or boiler, did they do what they were supposed to maintain them? In these two situations you lease with the landlord and your service contract with the service company will be vitally important in determining if they are responsible for what happened to you.

It will be important for you to know what caused your Carbon Monoxide Poisoning and whether anyone had a legal duty to you to prevent it. The legal duty part will have to be determined with the assistance of an attorney. Many times there will be people or entities that are responsible for what happened to you that you do not know about. That is why it is important to consult with an attorney to ensure that a complete a thorough investigation is performed.

Further, you will want to get a complete copy of all of your medical records related to your Carbon Monoxide Poisoning. These records will be invaluable to any attorney you consult with in determining whether or not you have a legitimate Carbon Monoxide Poisoning Case. If there was Police or Fire Department involvement in your Carbon Monoxide Poisoning you are also going to want to get copies of their reports as well. There is typically valuable information contained in those reports that will assist the attorney you consult with in determining whether or not you have a viable case.

If in your heart you believe that someone else is responsible for you being poisoned by Carbon Monoxide you owe it to yourself to contact an attorney. By contacting an attorney you will be able to discuss your specific situation and the facts surrounding how you were poisoned. They will be able to provide you with an evaluation of the case and let you know whether or not you really have a case. The worst case scenario is that after explaining the situation to the attorney and showing him the contracts, records and reports that you collected they tell you that they do not believe you have a case.

However, if the attorney investigates your potential case and is willing to take you on as a client, chances are there is a good basis for a lawsuit. Either way you have done yourself a service by investigating your legal rights.

CHAPTER VIII

What Is The Legal Process Like For A Carbon Monoxide Poisoning Lawsuit?

After gathering all of the facts and medical records available, your attorney will develop a litigation strategy for your specific case. This strategy should always focus on winning at trial. You see, if the attorney does not start from day one with the belief that your case is going to trial they won't be ready for trial in your case. This is not to say that settlement is not contemplated, but if settlement becomes the key focus, many nuances in the case that would be essential for winning your trial are missed. It is much easier to prepare for settlement if you have prepared to go to trial. In fact you chances for obtaining a favorable settlement are much stronger if you have prepared for trial, because the other side knows that you are not just using trial as a threat, you are fully ready to go to trial and have a jury decide the outcome. This is not something that many defendants, insurance company and defense attorneys like to think about.

Prior to filing the actual lawsuit your attorney may attempt to settle the case with the Defendant or their insurance company. There are benefits to you in this scenario, as the costs and fees of your attorney are typically less than after the filing of a lawsuit. However, the majority of the time Defendants or their insurance companies do not want to settle your claim without a lawsuit being filed. Many times Defendants and their insurance companies believe that any attempt to settle a case prior to the filing of a lawsuit is a sign of weakness. Most of the time this is far from the truth and these Defendants and Insurance Companies regret not making an effort to resolve a case before a lawsuit is filed. As Forrest Gump said "Stupid is, as Stupid does."

Once a lawsuit is filed, both sides will engage in a process known as discovery. This is basically a legal process in which both sides get to find out what the other is going to say and show at trial. The defendant will have access to your medical records, work history and income records. The defendant will be able to take you deposition under oath and you may be required to submit to a medical examination by a physician chosen by the Defendant.

Don't get the wrong idea, you and your attorney will be able to do discovery of your own as well. Your attorney will get records from the defendants and take deposition under oath of key people involved in the incident that resulted in your filing of a lawsuit. This is where all the facts, good, bad and ugly come to light and both sides get to evaluate them.

There are many reasons that a case settles during litigation. Many times, one or both sides realize that it would be in their best interest to resolve the case between themselves than to risk a jury making a decision that will not be favorable to them. Many times if a case settles before trial the costs of the case are significantly lower than they would have been if the case gone to trial and verdict.

It is important to remember that even the cases with the best facts; best clients sometimes don't do well at trial. A jury trial is a gamble, that sometimes is worth taking and other times is not worth taking. This is where an attorney will help you analyze the defendant's best offer and compare it to what you might net by going to trial.

Matthew E Mazur Jr.

CHAPTER IX

Before You Make An Appointment For That "Free Consultation"

Before you make an appointment with any attorney, you should ask them to send you written information about them and their law firm. You should ask for a sample fee agreement. You also want a full explanation of any potential fees and costs, the difference between the two, and how the fee is calculated in writing. Typically, this should be contained in the sample fee agreement they provide.

You also want to request written confirmation that they carry Malpractice Insurance. You would be shocked at the number of attorneys who do not carry any malpractice coverage. This is not a good thing for them or for you. Malpractice Insurance is a policy of insurance carried by attorneys in the event that they make a mistake. You want to hire attorneys who have Malpractice Insurance because if they make a mistake and it negatively impacts your case you want to make sure the Attorney has a way of covering the loss, they caused you.

You should also request a professional biography that outlines at a minimum, how long they have been actually going to trial. You want to make sure that you are retaining an attorney who has been to trial, knows what a courtroom is and is willing to go to trial if you case warrants it.

Take the time to do some investigation on the attorney before you hire them. Go to the State Bar Association website and look up the potential attorney. Find out whether or not they have ever had any disciplinary issues with the State Bar Association. Perform a Google search of them to see what information there is on the internet. Then meet with them, get to know them. See if you trust them. Remember this is one of the most important decisions you will make in your life. You want to make sure the attorney is someone that you want to work with and who will work hard for you and your family.

A special note about me and my law firm: if you are already represented by an attorney it is my personal policy not to take your case. If you are already represented by an attorney this book may have raised some questions in your mind. That is not a bad thing; it is actually good for both you and your case. Ask your current attorney these questions. It is important that you know what is going on in your case. Everyone does things a little differently and we do not accept cases in which another attorney is already involved because chances are they are not handling the case the way we would handle it and it is very difficult to take over a case that has already started. If you are currently represented, use this book to increase your understanding and knowledge to ask questions, but please do not ask me to take on your case. I won't do it.

Matthew E Mazur Jr.

CHAPTER X

What Cases Do You Not Accept?

With regard to Carbon Monoxide cases, they are very expensive to litigate so we have to carefully evaluate which cases we will take. The following are the types of cases we will not take.

• If you have been poisoned by Carbon Monoxide and have not sought any medical treatment, we will not accept your case.

• If you have been poisoned by Carbon Monoxide received medical treatment initially and then stopped receiving medical treatment for any reason other than you could not afford to continue it, we will not accept your case.

• If you have been poisoned by Carbon Monoxide received medical treatment initially and continue to receive medical treatment but are not following your physician's orders, taking your medication or missing appointments, we will not accept your case. Contrary to popular belief, your case will do better before a jury if you are actually trying to get better or overcome your condition. If you are not following doctor's orders, taking your medications or missing appointments jurors may think you are faking it. Don't give a jury a reason not give you the verdict you deserve. Follow your doctor's orders, take your medication and don't miss your medical appointments.

• If you have been poisoned by Carbon Monoxide and do not have tests showing your **CARBOXYHEMOGLOBIN** level at or close to the time of your poisoning, we will probably not take your case. Cases that fall under this scenario will be evaluated closely to determine if there are other factors that make it a case worth taking on.

- If you have had prior significant head injuries or trauma, chances are we will not take your case. Cases that fall under this scenario will be evaluated closely to determine if there are other factors that make it a case worth taking on.

- If you are the type of person who does not listen or take advice well, do us both a favor and do not contact us. You will save both of us a lot of stress and aggravation. I will only work with clients who will listen and take advice. There is a reason that you are hiring me and it is not because I am another pretty face. It is because I have training and experience in dealing with Carbon Monoxide Poisoning Cases. There will be times that you will not like what I am telling you, but you will realize very quickly if we work together that I do not sugar coat things and if I tell you something or give you advice it is for a reason.

- If we take your case and afterwards find out that you have lied to us, we will drop your case. We do not accept **our client's lying to us.** If you lie to us, we will drop you like a bad habit. Our reputation is on the line in every case we take and we will not risk our reputation on a liar. No matter the attorney you choose to represent you, please be honest with them. It is the best way for you to ensure a positive outcome in your case.

- If you are currently represented by another attorney, we will not take your case. To be honest with you the reason we do not take cases already started by other attorneys is because they handle them differently than we do. Many times, they do things that we would never have done, that are not to say what they have done is wrong, but it limits our ability to handle a case the way we want to handle it. We like to handle a case from the beginning so that we control its progress and develop the strategy for trial.

- Cases where the statute of limitations will soon run.

To properly evaluate a Carbon Monoxide Poisoning case takes time, if you come to us with a month left on the Statute of Limitations we just wouldn't be able to properly evaluate it in time to make a decision on whether or not to take on your case. If you are in this situation, feel free to contact us and we will recommend you to an attorney or two that may be able to help you out. Unfortunately, we will not be able to take your case.

If your case does not fail within one of these scenarios, please feel free to contact me to discuss your case. There may be other issues that impact our ability to take on your case. These issues will be discussed thoroughly with you and in the event that we decide not to take on your case we will provide you with the names of some other attorneys you can contact.

CHAPTER XI

The Eight Biggest Mistakes You Can Make That Will Poison Your Case

The following are the **EIGHT BIGGEST MISTAKES** that can poison your Carbon Monoxide Poisoning case.

1. You fail to seek medical attention upon finding out that you have been exposed to Carbon Monoxide. It does not look good to the defense attorney, insurance company, or jury if you are claiming medical injuries as a result of being poisoned by Carbon Monoxide and you never sought any medical treatment. If you think you were exposed to Carbon Monoxide go to the emergency room, get a carboxyhemoglobin test done. It is not enough to say that you have been poisoned by Carbon Monoxide, you need proof.

You may have all of the symptoms associated with Carbon Monoxide Poisoning, but if you do not have objective proof that you were in fact poisoned by Carbon Monoxide it makes winning you case very difficult. A good defense attorney will stand up before the jury and give them a ton of other reasons why you have the symptoms you do, but if you have a Carboxyhemoglobin Test that shows you were poisoned it makes the defense attorney's job a lot harder.

There are other objective tests as well that help to show that you have been poisoned by Carbon Monoxide. These tests provide even further proof to the jury, defense attorney and insurance company that your case is legitimate and you should be compensated.

2. You fail to continue with medical care following your initial visit to the emergency room or your doctor. This is not to say that you should seek out unnecessary medical care

and treatment. If you are truly a victim of Carbon Monoxide Poisoning you will not stop seeking medical care and treatment. You condition will require it.

We do not go into great detail on the specifics about the long-term symptoms of Carbon Monoxide Poisoning in this book for a reason. We do not want this book to be used to fabricate a Carbon Monoxide Case. Even though we believe that it is impossible to fabricate a Carbon Monoxide Case completely, there are individuals and unscrupulous attorneys who just might try it.

When we talk to prospective clients we listen carefully to their complaints and how they describe them, we know what Carbon Monoxide Poisoning complaints should sound like. If they don't sound right we don't take the case. One telltale sign of a marginal to bogus case is if a person stops going to the doctor for treatment following an exposure where they are claiming life altering symptoms. Financial situations do play a role in medical treatment, but it is relatively easy to figure out if someone is trying to pull a fast one.

If we suspect you are trying to pull one over on us, we are going to call you on it. We will drop any client we suspect of being dishonest with us regardless of the amount of money we invested into the case.

3. You exaggerate your symptoms or problems. This is human nature. If you are hurt and believe that someone else is responsible you want your case against them to go well. You might think consciously or unconsciously that you have to play up your problems or symptoms to make your case better. This could not be further from the truth. If you play up your symptoms or problems you are going to look like a faker. You are going to hurt your case and possibly damage it beyond repair. If you are truly suffering from the effects of Carbon Monoxide Poisoning you do not need to play up your

symptoms or problems. They will be obvious in your medical records and in the course your life has taken since you were poisoned.

Defense Attorneys and Insurance Companies routinely hire private investigators to conduct video surveillance. Now, they also troll YouTube, MySpace, Facebook, other social networking sites or Google you to find out what you are up to. If you claim that you cannot run, climb or stoop, and you get caught on video or brag about breaking a personal running record on MySpace you can forget about your lawsuit.

There is really no explanation other then, you videotaped my twin brother that can overcome the eye of the camera. Don't make a good case bad by playing up symptoms or problems. Don't give the Defense Attorney the easy argument that you are a malingerer or faker. Don't let a surveillance video prove to a jury that you are a liar. Juries don't like having their time wasted and if they think you are faking you are wasting their time and their verdict will reflect that.

4. You fail to keep a journal of how your life has changes since you were poisoned by Carbon Monoxide. Some attorneys cringe when they see this as they are afraid of it getting into the hands of the defense attorney. This is exactly what we want to happen. If you keep a daily journal of things that are going on in your life that are different than they were before you were poisoned you will help to tell your story better for the jury, defense attorney and Insurance company. If you are truly hurt, this journal will be vital to ensuring your entire story gets told.

One of the known long-term effects of Carbon Monoxide Poisoning is memory problems. Things may occur to you on a daily basis that you won't remember at the time of your deposition, but if you take the time to write them down as they happen you will have preserved them. Additionally, this journal will also be invaluable to your treating medical providers because a lot of times the information they need may not be readily remembered by you at an appointment. You can share with them your journal entries to make sure they are getting an accurate picture of your condition.

It would also be helpful if your spouse or parents made entries as well, as there are things they are going to notice that you most likely will not. Their observations are not only vital to your case but also to your medical care and treatment, which is more important than your case. Remember no matter what happens in your Carbon Monoxide lawsuit, win, lose, or draw you will still be dealing with the lifelong effects of Carbon Monoxide Poisoning. That is way it is important to make sure that your medical providers are getting the full picture so that your symptoms can be managed in such a way as to allow you to live your life to its fullest potential.

5. You hide past accidents from your attorney. Once you begin your case, the defense will be interested in knowing about any past accidents you may have had. The reality is that they probably already know they answer or have easy access to that information. All insurance companies subscribe to insurance databases and often the only reason that you are asked about prior accidents is to see if you are an honest person

If you have been in other accidents, you attorney needs to know about them so that they can investigate them to see if they will become a problem in your case. If you do not let them know about prior accidents or you misrepresent you prior accident history to your attorney or to the Defense you will almost guarantee that you will lose your case.

6. You hide other injuries or conditions you have from

your attorney. It goes without saying that you should be upfront with your attorney about any injuries or conditions you had before or after the incident which is the basis of your lawsuit. Again, if you saw a doctor or other healthcare provider, then there is a record in existence that the Defense will find. Your attorney can deal with this if they know about it. If you lie about it, and the Defense finds out, then your case is more likely than not over. Remember, there is no privacy in America today. When you file a lawsuit, your life becomes an open book.

If you are a client of mine and your doctor keeps "two sets of records" because they have been treating you for years and you do not make sure that we get **ALL OF YOUR RECORDS**, we will fire you as a client.

7. You do not have accurate tax returns. In almost every case, a client will have lost income because of being poisoned by Carbon Monoxide. You will only be able to claim that lost income if you past tax returns are pristine. You do not want to risk going to jail by claiming a loss of income, only to have your past tax returns not back up your claim. Again, being honest with your attorney is the only way to be, because they can deal with the problem if they know about it.

Be aware that you will most likely be required to produce your tax returns if you file a lawsuit and claim lost wages. If you are a liar and a cheat, this will come back to haunt you in your case. If you are thinking of retaining me as your attorney be aware that I won't associate with liars and cheats and if I find out that there are issues with your taxes that you did not inform me about up front I will fire you as a client, regardless of how much money I have invested in your case.

8. You lose hope. Many times, during litigation a client loses hope. They ask themselves "why did I ever file this lawsuit?" They begin to think that they would be better off

walking away and forgetting the whole thing. When this happens to you, take a moment to reflect on why you filed your lawsuit. Realize that the reason you filed your lawsuit is because someone did something that hurt you and you have to deal with the results of their actions for the rest of your life. A lawsuit is not an easy road. There will be ups and downs. There will be good days and bad. You cannot lose hope. You have to believe in yourself and your cause. Do yourself a favor when this happens, and it happens to every client, call your attorney up and talk to them. Tell them how you are feeling and get reassurance from them. Remember your attorney believes in you and your cause or they would have never taken your case.

CHAPTER XII

Internet Resources On Carbon Monoxide Poisoning

The following are links to useful online resources related to Carbon Monoxide Poisoning. This list is not extensive, but it does provide you with some quality resources to help you on your quest for information.

1. www.carbonmonoxidehelp.com – This is our firm's Carbon Monoxide website. It has useful information regarding Carbon Monoxide Poisoning and litigation.

2. www.carbonmonoxidekills.com – This is a great general information website on Carbon Monoxide and Carbon Monoxide Poisoning. It is based out of the United Kingdom, but most of the information provided is useful anywhere around the world.

3. www.cdc.gov/co/faqs.htm - This website is maintained by the Centers for Disease Control and provides valuable information about Carbon Monoxide Poisoning. It is a great site to increase your understanding about Carbon Monoxide Poisoning.

4. www.epa.gov/iaq/pubs/coftsht.html - This website is maintained by the Environmental Protection Agency. It is a great resource for Carbon Monoxide Poisoning prevention.

5. www.cdc.gov/co/boating.htm - This is another part of the CDC website that deals with Carbon Monoxide Poisoning and boating. It has very useful and important information if you are a boater and have concerns about Carbon Monoxide Poisoning.

6. www.uscgboating.org/recalls/pdfs/COflyer.pdf - This is a link to a flyer produced by the U.S. Coast Guard on Carbon Monoxide Poisoning risks and boating. It is very informative and should be reviewed if you own a boat.

7. www.emergency.com/co2poisn.htm - Is a website for Emergency Physicians that as useful information about Carbon Monoxide Poisoning.

8. www.bbc.co.uk/health/conditions/carbonmonoxide1.shtml - Is a website run by British Broadcasting and it has good general information about Carbon Monoxide Poisoning.

9. www.med.umich.edu/1libr/aha/aha_carbmono_crs.htm - A website run by the University of Michigan. It has good information about Carbon Monoxide Poisoning.

10. www.chm.bris.ac.uk/motm/co/coh.htm - This website is maintained by Dr. Mike Thompson of Winchester College in the United Kingdom. It has a great visual of a Carbon Monoxide molecule and useful information about Carbon Monoxide.

11. www.rad.usuhs.edu/medpix/medpix.html?mode=single&recnum=7501&table=card&srchstr=carbon This website provide you with imaging of the effects of Carbon Monoxide on the brain.

12. www.extension.iastate.edu/Pages/communications/CO/ - This website is operated by Iowa State University and provide good overall information on Carbon Monoxide Poisoning.

13. www.ispub.com/ostia/index.php?xmlFilePath=journals/ijto/vol1n1/CO.xml - This website is a must read. It provides useful information on Car-

bon Monoxide Poisoning from a Toxicological prospective.

14.   www.mayoclinic.com/health/carbon-monoxide/DS00648 - This website is maintained by the Mayo Clinic. It is a great resource for information on Carbon Monoxide Poisoning.

15.   http://www.coheadquarters.com/CO1.htm - This web site is maintained by Dr. David G. Penny, Ph.D. He is a Professor of Physiology at Wayne State University School of Medicine, Detroit, Michigan, and is the Director of Surgical Research at Providence Hospital in Southfield, Michigan. This site has good information on Carbon Monoxide Poisoning. This website is a must read if you are interested in expanding your knowledge of Carbon Monoxide Poisoning.

For even more resources beyond those listed here we highly recommend that you Google "Carbon Monoxide Poisoning." There are literally thousands of websites around the world that have valuable and useful information on Carbon Monoxide Poisoning. Do yourself a favor and take some time to do some research on Carbon Monoxide Poisoning before you contact an attorney, that way you will have a basic understanding and will know if they are trying to pull one over on you. The last thing you want to do is retain an attorney who does not have a good working knowledge of Carbon Monoxide Poisoning and lacks experience in handling Carbon Monoxide Poisoning cases.

Matthew E Mazur Jr.

About our Firm

We Don't Take Every Case That Comes Through The Door –

This Means We Have More Time For Your Case.

Our firm is not your typical law firm; we don't take every case that comes through the door. We don't rely on a high volume of cases generated by gigantic television, radio and Yellow Page advertising. We do not claim to handle every type of law under the sun. Quite frankly, we do not want to handle every type of law under the sun because we do not need to.

We are not a television personal injury mill. Every year, we accept a limited number of carbon monoxide cases from the people who ask us to represent them. By not taking every case we have more time for your case, and we believe this gives us the ability to achieve better results overall.

Sometime the best advice you can get when you are contemplating filing a lawsuit is that you do not have a claim that can be won. If after reviewing you case, we find this to be true, we will tell you. However, if after we review you case and we decide to accept it, you can be assured that you will receive the personal attention you deserve. We will represent you aggressively, keep you up to date on what is happening in your case, and give you advice as to whether you should settle your case or go to trial.

If you would like more information, visit our website at www.carbonmonoxidehelp.com. On our website you will find additional useful information, as well as our Carbon Monoxide Help Blog, which contains current information on Carbon Monoxide Poisoning incidents, cases, medical treatments, and commentary. If you would like to speak to one of our attorneys, please feel free to call us at (305) 466-3328 or e-mail us at info@mazur-law.com.

We will explain all of the fees and costs to you fully before we start working on your case. Together, as a team, we will decide on the best tactics for your case.

Matthew E. Mazur, Jr., Esq.

Weston, Florida